Let's Joke Around!

LET'S TELL JOKES ABOUT SNAKES

Leonard Clasky

WINDMILL BOOKS™

Published in 2023 by Windmill Books, an Imprint of Rosen Publishing
2544 Clinton St., Buffalo, NY 14224

Disclaimer: Portions of this work were originally authored by Maria Nelson and published as *Jokes and More About Snakes*. All new material in this edition authored by Leonard Clasky.

Editor: Caitie McAneney
Book Design: Rachel Rising

Photo Credits: Cover, p. 4 Eric Isselee/Shutterstock.com; cover, pp. 1, 3-24 V_ctoria/Shutterstock.com; p. 5 Lauren Suryanata/Shutterstock.com; pp. 6, 8, 10, 12, 14, 16, 18, 20, 22 HappyPictures/Shutterstock.com; p. 7 Kurit afshen/Shutterstock.com; p. 9 DedeDian/Shutterstock.com; p. 11 Harris Motion Photo/Shutterstock.com; p. 13 Egoreichenkov Evgenii/Shutterstock.com; p. 15 Karel Bartik/Shutterstock.com; p. 17 thomaslabriekl/Shutterstock.com; p. 19 Susan M Jackson/Shutterstock.com; p. 21 lisdiyanto suhardjo/Shutterstock.com.

Cataloging-in-Publication Data
Names:Clasky, Leonard.
Title: Let's tell jokes about snakes / Leonard Clasky.
Description: New York : Windmill Books, 2023. | Series: Lets's Joke Around!| Includes glossary.
Identifiers: ISBN 9781538392973 (pbk.) | ISBN 9781538392980 (library bound) | ISBN 9781538392997 (ebook)
Subjects: LCSH: Jokes –Juvenile literature. | Snakes, humor –Juvenile literature
Classification: LCC PN6231.S6 C53 2023 | DDC 818/.602–dc23

Manufactured in the United States of America

CPSIA Compliance Information: Batch #CWWM23. For further information contact Rosen Publishing at 1-800-237-9932.

Find us on

CONTENTS

SCARED SILLY

A fear of snakes is one of the most common **phobias** in the world, and it's no wonder—some can eat people and large animals whole! Some, like the cobra and black mamba, kill **prey** with **venomous** bites. Others, like pythons, wind around their prey and squeeze it so it can't breathe.

However, only about 7 percent of the world's 3,000 snake **species** can kill or seriously harm a person. Many of them aren't venomous at all. Can these slithering snakes be silly? Let's find out!

BALL PYTHON

SOME SNAKES, LIKE BALL PYTHONS, DON'T HAVE VENOM OR EVEN **FANGS**. OTHER SNAKES, LIKE THIS KING COBRA, ARE VERY VENOMOUS!

KING COBRA

SNAKE SNACKS

WHAT DO YOU CALL A SNAKE WHO LIKES DESSERT?
A pie-thon.

WHAT DO YOU GET IF YOU CROSS A HOT DOG WITH A SNAKE?
A fang-furter.

WHAT DID THE SNAKE SAY WHEN IT WAS OFFERED A PIECE OF CAKE?
"Sure, but just a slither."

WHAT DID THE PYTHON
SAY TO ITS PREY?

I've got a crush on you.

SNAKE SCHOOL

WHAT'S A SNAKE'S FAVORITE SUBJECT?
Hissstory.

WHY DID THE SNAKE DO SO WELL IN MATH CLASS?
It was an adder.

WHY COULDN'T THE SNAKE TALK IN CLASS?
It had a frog in its throat.

SNAKES ON THE MOVE

WHICH STATE DO SNAKES LIKE TO VISIT FOR VACATION?
Hiss-issippi.

WHY ARE SNAKES HARD TO TRICK?
You can't pull their leg.

WHAT DID THE SNAKE PACK FOR ITS HUNTING TRIP?
A boa and arrow.

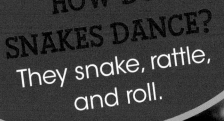

SNAKES WITH A TWIST

WHAT DO YOU GET WHEN YOU CROSS A TUBA AND A SNAKE?
A snake in the brass.

WHAT DO YOU GET WHEN YOU CROSS A COMPUTER WITH A PYTHON?
A mega-bite.

WHAT DO YOU GET WHEN A SHEEP, A DRUM, AND A SNAKE ALL RUN INTO EACH OTHER?
Baa-dum-tsss.

SNAKES AT WORK

WHAT KIND OF SNAKE IS THE BEST AT CLEANING CARS?
A windshield viper.

WHAT KIND OF SNAKE WORKS FOR THE GOVERNMENT?
A civil **serpent**.

WHAT SHOULD SNAKES WEAR TO THE OFFICE?
A boa tie.

WHAT KIND OF SNAKE LIKES TO BUILD THINGS?
A boa constructor.

SNAKES IN LOVE

HOW DO SNAKES END A FIGHT?
They hiss and make up.

WHAT IS A SNAKE LOOKING FOR IN A PARTNER?
A good poisonality.

WHAT DO YOU CALL A COBRA WITH A GREAT PERSONALITY?
A snake charmer.

SNAKE TROUBLE!

WHAT HAPPENS WHEN A SNAKE GETS ANGRY?
They have a hissy fit.

WHAT DO YOU GIVE A SICK SNAKE?
Asp-rin.

HOW DID THE BOA GET BACK THE MONEY HE LOANED HIS FRIEND?
He put the squeeze on him!

SNAKES WITH STYLE

WHAT KIND OF SLIPPERS DO SNAKES WEAR?
Water moccasins.

WHAT'S A SNAKE'S FAVORITE DANCE?
The mamba.

WHAT DID THE SNAKE BUY FOR ITS KITCHEN?
New rep-tiles.

WHY DO BABIES LIKE DIAMONDBACKS?

Because they come with their own rattle.

FUN SNAKE FACTS!

- Snakes shed their skin every few months as they grow.

- Some snakes can "fly." They flatten their bodies and slither in an S shape as they glide through the air.

- Not all legless reptiles are snakes. Some lizards have only front or back legs or may have no legs at all!

- Snakes eat their prey live! They also eat it whole, or without chewing it up.

- Snakes have super **senses**. They can "hear" sound waves through their jaw, smell with their tongue, and "see" heat from warm-blooded prey.

GLOSSARY

asp: A venomous snake in Egypt, usually known to be a cobra.

fang: A long, pointed tooth.

personality: A creature's nature and ways of acting.

phobia: A very strong fear or dislike of something.

prey: An animal that is hunted by other animals for food.

sense: Any of five ways to understand or experience one's surroundings.

serpent: Another word for snake.

species: A group of plants or animals that are all the same kind.

venomous: Containing venom, a poison an animal makes in its body.

FOR MORE INFORMATION

Books

Davies, Monica. *Deadly Pythons*. New York, NY: Gareth Stevens Publishing, 2023.

Humphrey, Natalie. *Boa Constrictor: Ready to Squeeze*. New York, NY: Enslow Publishing, 2022.

Websites

Awesome 8: Super Snakes

kids.nationalgeographic.com/nature/article/super-snakes

Explore some exciting facts about super snakes!

Snakes

www.dkfindout.com/us/animals-and-nature/reptiles/snakes/

Learn more about snakes, including their body parts and features.